ARTIST TRANSCRIPTIONS® PIANO

JAZZ PIANO MASTERS PLAY
Rodgers & Hammerstein

T0080141

Cover photo courtesy Photofest

ISBN 978-1-4803-6853-8

WILLIAMSON MUSIC®

AN IMAGEM COMPANY™
www.rnh.com

HAL•LEONARD®
CORPORATION
7777 W. Bluemound Rd. P.O. Box 13819 Milwaukee, WI 53213

Visit Hal Leonard Online at
www.halleonard.com

DISCOGRAPHY

Bali Ha'i
from JANE JARVIS TRIO: CUT GLASS

Getting to Know You
from MULGREW MILLLER: GETTING TO KNOW YOU

Happy Talk
from MONTY ALEXANDER TRIO: FULL STEAM AHEAD

Hello, Young Lovers
from ERIC REED: PURE IMAGINATION

I Have Dreamed
from JON MAYER: MY ROMANCE

It Might As Well Be Spring
from BILL EVANS TRIO: MOONBEAMS

My Favorite Things
from DAVE BRUBECK: MY FAVORITE THINGS

Oh, What a Beautiful Mornin'
from JOE LOVANO AND HANK JONES: KIDS: LIVE AT DIZZY'S CLUB

People Will Say We're in Love
from ROGER KELLAWAY: SINGIN' IN THE RAIN

Shall We Dance?
from GERALD WIGGINS TRIO: THE KING AND I

The Sound of Music
from ANDRE PREVIN: GIVE MY REGARDS TO BRODAWAY

The Surrey with the Fringe on Top
from WYNTON KELLY: COMPLETE VEE JAY STUDIO RECORDINGS

This Nearly Was Mine
from DICK HYMAN PLAYS VARIATIONS ON RICHARD RODGERS

We Kiss in a Shadow
from RED GARLAND: ROJO

Younger than Springtime
from OSCAR PETERSON: DIGITAL AT MONTREUX

CONTENTS

Bali Ha'i

from *SOUTH PACIFIC*

Lyrics by Oscar Hammerstein II
Music by Richard Rodgers

G7♭9
C7(add4) E7♭9/C Fmaj7
Fdim7(add9)
F9
G13♭9 G7♯5(♭9) C9♯5 C7♯5(♭9) Fmaj7
D7
G7♭9
C7♭9
F7♯9
E♭9 D7
G7♭9
C7(add4) E7♭9/C F7
B♭13
F7♯9
B♭13
F7♯9 B♭13
D7♯9
A13
D7♯9
Gm
D9

Gm6 F♯dim7 Gm
B♭m
B♭m6
C7
Fdim7(add9)
F9
G13♭9 G7♯5(♭9) C9♯5 C7♯5(♭9) Fmaj7
G7♭9
C7♭9
F13♭5
E♭9
D7♯9
Piano Solo - Chorus 1
G7♭9
C7(add4) E13♭9/C F6
cresc.
f
Fdim7(9) Fdim(maj7) Fdim7(9)
mp
Fdim(maj7)
Fdim7(9) Fdim(maj7) Fdim
E♭7 Dm7 D♭m7 C7

F7♯9
E7
E♭9♯11
D13♯11
D♭9
C7♯5
F
Fdim7
C7♯5
F7
Fdim7
F7
Fdim7
F7♯9
F7
C7
F7
Fdim7
Edim7
E♭dim7
D7♯9
C♭maj7/D♭
D♭9
C9
E7/C
F7
N.C.
8va
loco
B♭13
F9
B♭(♯9)
F9
B♭7
D9
E♭9
D9

D7♯9
Gm
6
Am7
Gm
Gm(maj7)
B♭m7
C7
F
Fm6/9
F9
C9
F6
C9
F7
Fdim7(maj9)
E7
E♭9
D7
D7♯9
A♭m9
D♭7
C7
F13(♯9)
N.C.
f

Solo - Chorus 2
F7♯9
C7♯5(♯9)
F7♯9
C7♯5(♯9)
F9
C7♯9
Fdim7
(13)
C7♯5(♯9)
F7
F9(♯9)
F13♭5
E7
E13♯11
E♭9
D7♭9
D♭9
C7
E7/C
F7
dim.
Fdim7
p
cresc.
Fm9♭5
E7
E♭7
ff

D7
D♭9
C7♯5(♯9)
C7♯5
F6/9
dim.
B♭9
E♭9
mp
B♭9
D9
Am7♭5
D7
Gm
Am7
D9
cresc.
Gm
B♭m
C
f
8va
loco
Fdim7
mf
F9
F7♯9
C7
F13

Fdim7(9)
Edim7(9)
E♭dim7(maj13)
D13♭5(♯9)
(♭9)
D♭7♯9
C7♯9
C7♯5
F13
dim.
Bass Solo
Fdim7
F7♯9
pp
F13
F7
29
(Comp under bass solo)
29
f
Piano Solo
F7♯9
B♭7♭9
F7♯9
D♭9
C7♯5
F7
F9
E7
A7
D7

D♭7
C7
F7
Fdim7
C7♯5(♯9)
Fdim7(13)
C13♯5(♭9)
F7♯9
Fdim7(9)
F9
G7♭9
C7♭9
F9
E9♯11
D♭9
D9♭5
D♭9
C7♯5(♭9)
E13♭9/C
F6
N.C.
Head (2nd half)
B♭13
D+(♯4)
Gm
D7
Gm6

Db9
C7#5(b9)
F7b9
mp
F7
Bb/C
F7#9
N.C.
F7#9
p
E7#9
A13(b9)
D7#9
Db9
C7#5
F
D7
Tag
G7b9
C7
E7b9/C
F7
Eb13
D13
cresc.
G7b9
f
C7
E7b9/C
F13
N.C.

Getting To Know You

from *THE KING AND I*

Lyrics by Oscar Hammerstein II
Music by Richard Rodgers

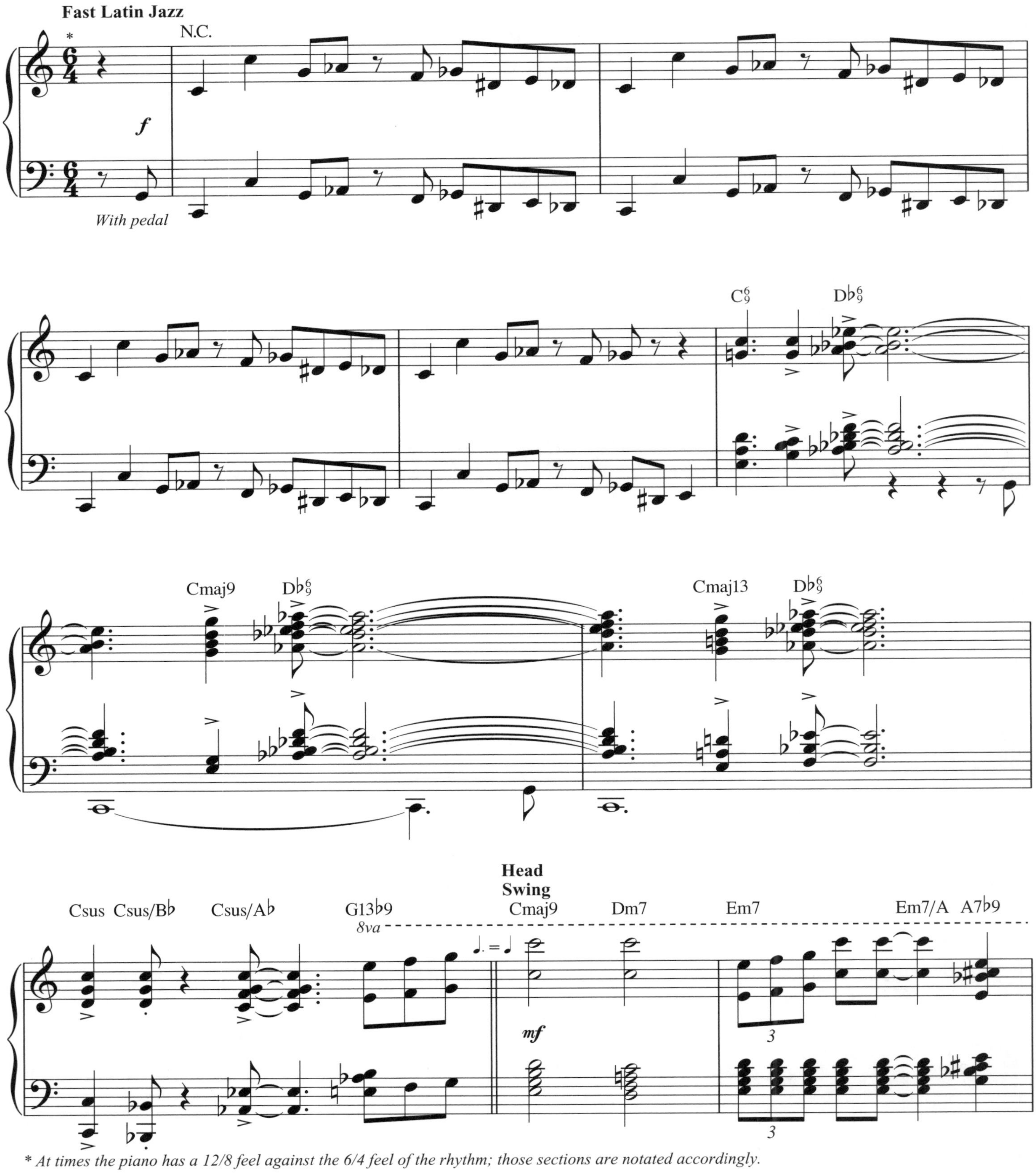

* *At times the piano has a 12/8 feel against the 6/4 feel of the rhythm; those sections are notated accordingly.*

Dm11 Em7 Fmaj7 Em7 A9 Dm7 Em7
(8va)
Fmaj7 G13 C6/9 B♭ A A♭ A B♭ Gmaj7
loco
G♭maj7 Fmaj7 Emaj7 G13♭9 Cmaj7 Dm7 Em7 A7♭9
8va
F Edim7 E♭9♯11 D7sus Am11 Am11(maj7)
(8va)
loco
Am7/D Dm9 F Dm7/A Dm7/G B♭m7/E♭ A♭maj7 Amaj9/B

D♭maj7
E♭m13
Em7
Am7
Dm7
Em7(4)
Fmaj7
Em7
E♭9♯11
8va
Dm9
Fmaj7
loco
G13
G7♭5(♭9)
C6/9
C/A♭
D♭/A
E♭/B
Bsus2/D♯
B♭sus2/D
Asus2/C♯
G7
F
Em11
A7
Dm7
(add4)
G(add2)
G13♭9(add11)
Bm11
E13
Dm9
N.C.
C6
F♯9
Fmaj7
A♭maj7/B♭

N.C.
Em11
F♯m(add4)
Dm7/G
Fm7/B♭
D13
Dm7/G
G13♭5(♭9)
Latin
N.C.
f
Piano Solo
D♭6/9
C6/9
D♭6/9
C6/9
D♭6/9

C6/9 D♭6/9 C6/9 D♭6/9
C6/9 D♭6/9 C6/9 D♭6/9
C6/9 D♭6/9 C6/9 D♭6/9 C6/9 D♭6/9
C6/9 D♭6/9 C6/9 D♭6/9 C6/9 D♭6/9
C6/9 D♭6/9 C6/9 D♭6/9

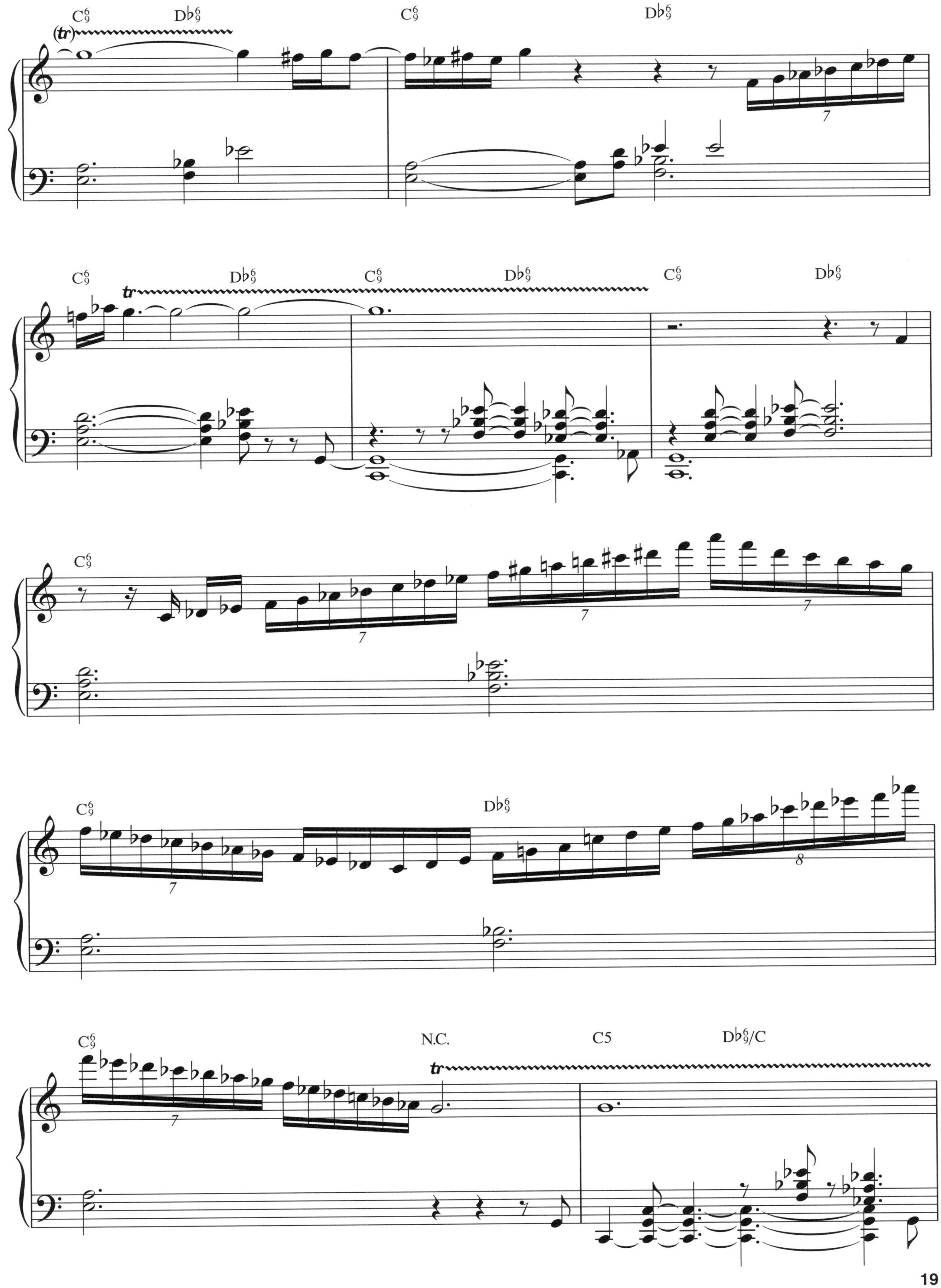
C6/9
D♭6/9
(tr)
tr
7
N.C.
C5
D♭6/9/C
8

C5
D♭6/9/C
(tr)
R.H.
C5
G♭maj13/C
C6/9
Fm11
N.C.
G13♭9
8va
Swing
C
Dm7
mf
Em7
(8va)
A7♯5
Dm7
Em7
Fmaj7
loco
Em7
Dm7
3
3
F/G
G13
Em7
A7♭9

Dm9
G7
C6/9
Dm7
Em7
C7
F
A7♯5(♯9)
E♭9
D9
Am9
Am(maj7)
D13
D9♯5
Dm7
A♭13
Fmaj7/G
G7♯5(♯9)
C
Dm7
Em7
A7
Dm7
A7♯5
Dm9
Em7♭5
Em7♭5/A
Dm9
G13
G7♯5(♯9)
8va
loco

Gm7
C7
Fmaj7
Em7
E♭7
Dm6/9
C7
A7♭9
F
G13♭9
C
G♭13
Fmaj9
A♭/B♭
Em7
Am9
D13
D13♯11
Dm9
G13♭9
Latin
N.C.
f

Cm7(add4)
N.C.
Fm9
Cm(add4)
G7♯5(♯9)

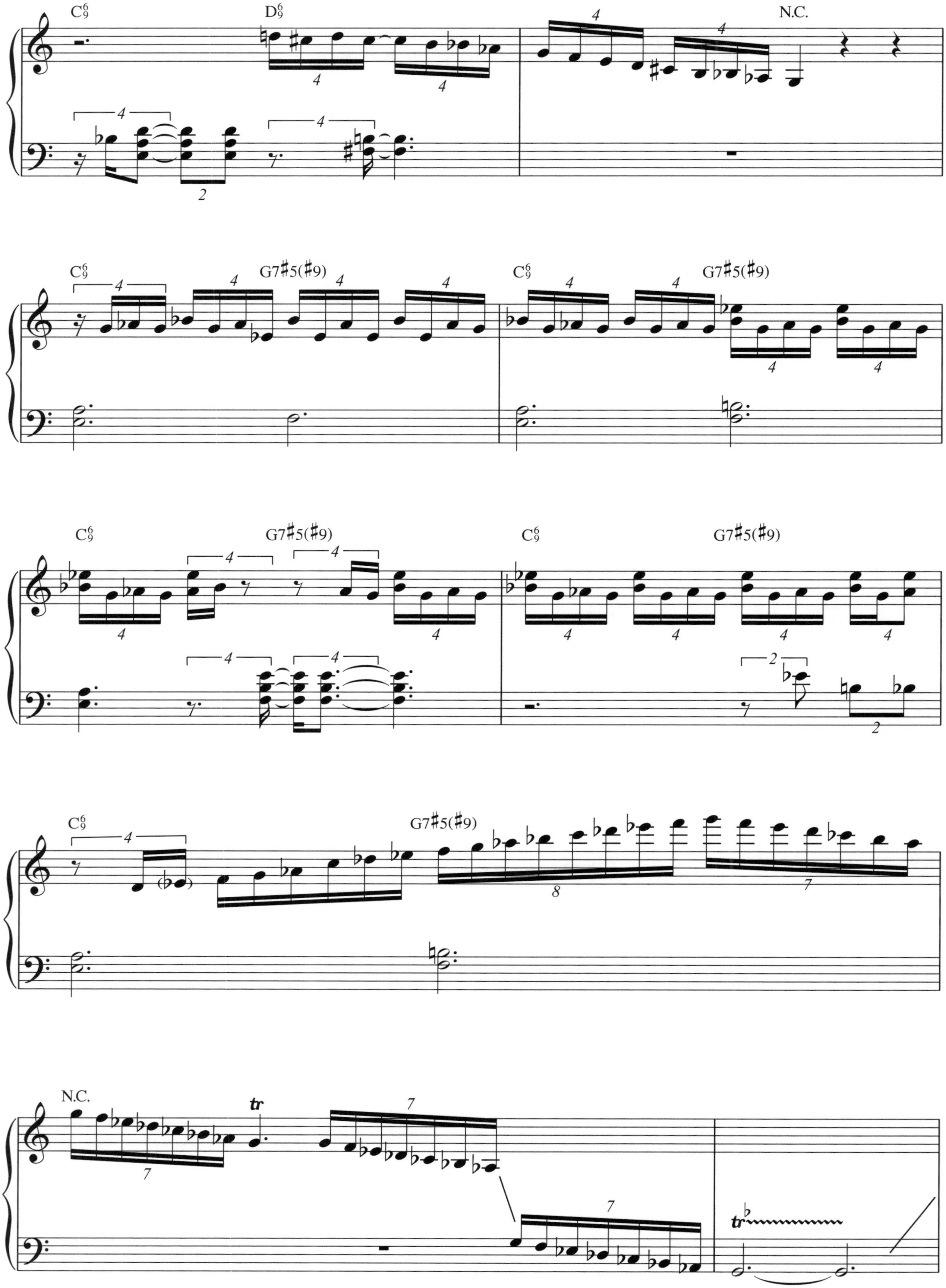
C6/9
D6/9
N.C.
C6/9
G7♯5(♯9)
C6/9
G7♯5(♯9)
C6/9
G7♯5(♯9)
C6/9
G7♯5(♯9)
C6/9
G7♯5(♯9)
N.C.
tr

8va
C6/9 G7♯5(♯9)
(8va)
C6/9 G7♯5(♯9)
C6/9 G7♯5(♯9)
N.C.
loco
G13♭9
8va
Head
Swing
Cmaj9 Dm7 Em7 Em7/A A7♭9
mf
Dm11 Em7 Fmaj7 Em7 A7 Dm7 Em7
(8va)

Fmaj7
G13
(8va)
C6
B♭maj7
Amaj7
A♭maj7
Amaj7
B♭maj7
Gmaj7
loco
G♭maj7
Fmaj7
Emaj7
G13♭9
8va
Cmaj9
Dm7
Em7
A7♭9
Gm/A
Fmaj7
Em11♭5
A7
E♭7♭5(♯9)
D7
Am11
Am11(maj7)
Am7/D
Dm9
F
Dm7/A
(8va)
loco
Dm7/G
B♭m7/E♭
A♭maj7
Amaj9/B
D♭maj7
E♭m13
Em7
Am7
Dm7
Em7
Fmaj7
Em7
A7
Dm9
Dm9(maj7)
Straight

Fmaj7
G13
C6
C/A♭
D♭/A
E♭/B
Bsus2/D♯
B♭sus2/D
Asus2/C♯
G7
F
Em11
A7
Dm7
G7
Bm11
E13
Dm11
N.C.
C6
F♯9
Fmaj7
A♭maj7/B♭
N.C.
Em11
F♯m(add4)
Dm7/G
Fm7/B♭
D13
D13♯11
Fmaj7/G
G7
Latin
N.C.
f

5
3 3 3 3
Cm7 D♭maj7/C Cm7 D♭maj7/C
8va
Cm7 D♭maj7/C Cm7 D♭maj7/C
Cm7 D♭maj7/C Cm7 D♭maj7/C
(8va)
Cm7 D♭maj7/C Cm7 D♭maj7/C
N.C.
8va

Happy Talk

from *SOUTH PACIFIC*

Lyrics by Oscar Hammerstein II
Music by Richard Rodgers

Gm7 C/G Gm9 C/G Gm11 C13♭9 D7♭5(♭9) D♭7♭5(♭9)
C7♭5(♭9) B7♭5(♭9) B9 B♭maj7 B♭m9 8va E♭9 loco
Fsus2/A E♭9♯11 D7♯5(♭9) 8va G13
Gm11 C7♯5 F A♭13 D♭maj13 G♭9♯11
F6 A/B B9 B♭13♯11

Am9
D9
Gm11
C7b9
D7#5(#9)
G7#5
Cm9
B9
Bb6
Bbm9
8va
3
Eb9
F6/A
A7#5
D7#5(b9)
G13
Gm7
C7
F6
Ab7
Db13
C7#5(b9)
Piano Solo - Chorus 1
F6
B9
Bb7#9
f

B♭7
D7♭9
Gm7
mf
C7♭9
Dm7
G7♯5
Cm9
F13♭9
B♭maj9
B♭6
B♭m7
E♭9
3
Am7
D7
G9
C9
3
3
Am7
3
D7
G7♯5
C7♯9

F13
B9
B♭9
E♭7
D7♭9
Gm7
C7♭9
Dm7
G7
C7
F7
B♭
B♭m7
B♭m7/E♭
Am7

D7♯9
D9
G9
Gm7(add4)
Fsus2/A
D7♯5(♯9)
D♭13
C7♯5(♯9)
Chorus 2
F
f
B9
B♭13♯11
A7♯5
D7♭9
G9
Gm9
Gm7/C
Am7/D
G7
Cm9
F13
B♭6
mf

B♭m7
E♭9
Am7
E♭m9
A♭13
G9
C7sus
F6
D7♯5
G9
C7sus
mp
F6
B9
B♭9
A7♯5
D7♭9

G9
D7♯5(♭9)
Gm7
C7
D7
G7
cresc.
Cm7
F7♯9
f
B♭9
B♭m9
E♭13
Am9
D13
F♯dim
Gm7
C7
Fmaj7
Em7♭5
A7
D7

Chorus 3
C7sus
F13
B9
f
B♭7♯9
A7♭5
D7
G9
Gm7
C9
D7♯9
G7♯5
3
Cm9
F13♭9
3
3
B♭9
B♭m7
E♭9
A7♭5
D7♯5

G7♭5(♯9)
3
Gm7/C
A7♯5(♭9)
D7♯5(♯9)
cresc.
G9
C7♯5(♯9)
F13
ff
B9♭5
B13
B♭9
A7♯5(♯9)
E♭7♯9
D7♯5(♯9)
G9
mf
Gm7/C
F/A
G7♯5
Cm9
F13♭9
B♭6/9
E♭9

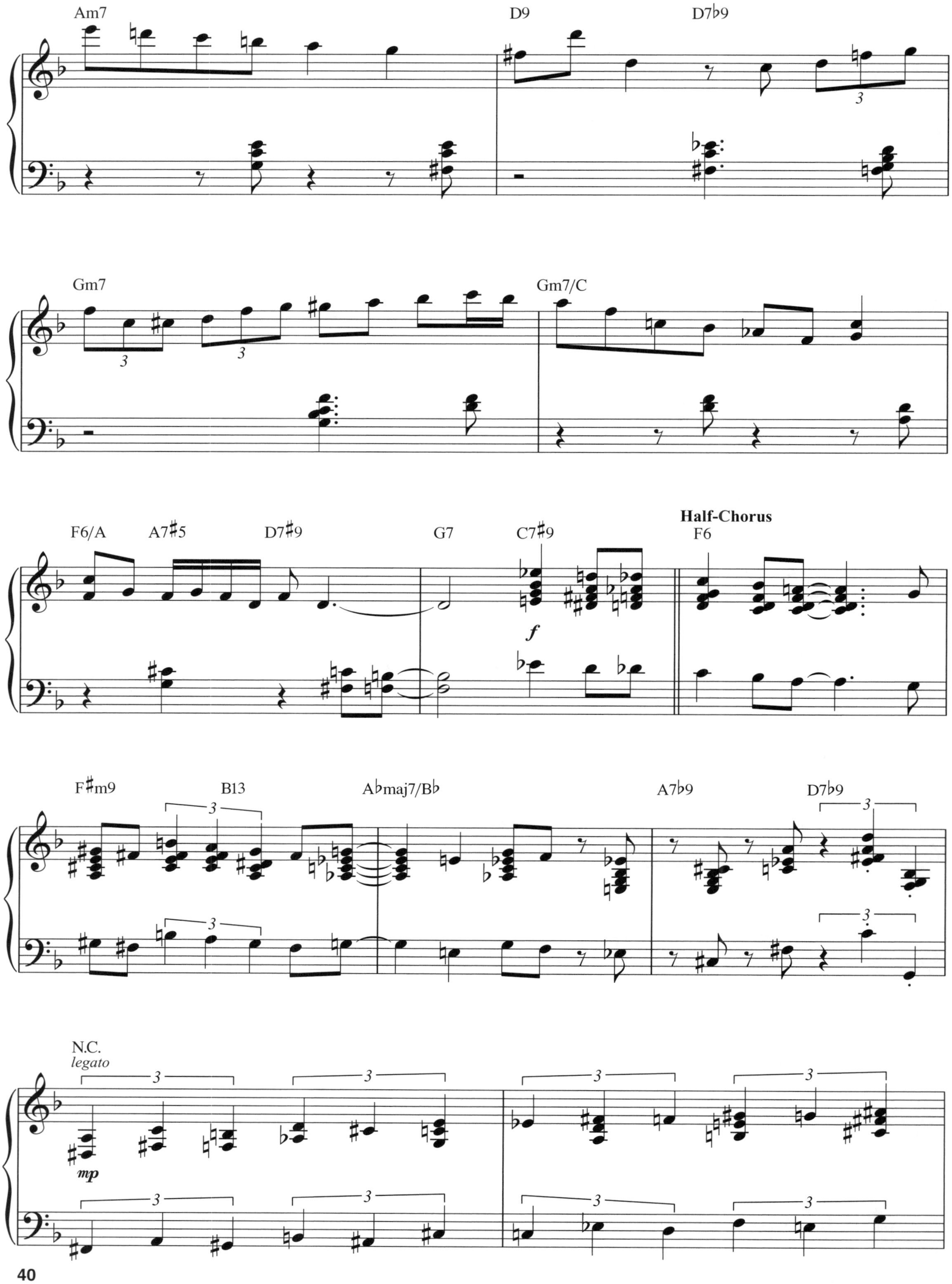
Am7
D9
D7♭9
3
Gm7
3
3
Gm7/C
F6/A
A7♯5
D7♯9
G7
C7♯9
f
Half-Chorus
F6
F♯m9
B13
3
A♭maj7/B♭
A7♭9
D7♭9
3
3
3
N.C.
legato
3
3
mp
3
3
3
3
3
3

cresc.
B♭13
f
B♭m6/9
A7♯5(♯9)
D7♯5(♯9)
G9
Gm7
C7
F/A
D7♯5(♯9)
G9
Gm7/C
Bass Solo
F6/9
B9♭5
dim.
p
N.C.
C7♯5(♯11)
28
(Comp under bass solo)
pp
ff

F13
B9♯5
B♭6/9
mf
A13
D7♯5(♯9)
G7
Gm7
C7
D7♭7
G7♭5
C7♭5
F7♭5(♭9)
B♭13♯11
N.C.
Drum solo
6
f
F13
Drum solo ends
B9
mf
B♭(add2)

E♭9
D7♯9
G9
C13
D7♯5(♭9)
G7sus
Cm7
F7
B♭
N.C.
Drum solo
Drum solo ends
Head
F13
B9
B♭13♯11
Am9
D9
D13♭9
Gm7
C/G
Gm9
C/G

Gm11
C13
D7♭5(♭9)
D♭9
C7♭5(♭9)
B9
B♭maj9
B♭m9
8va
E♭9
A7♯5(♯9)
E♭13♯11
D7♯5(♭9)
8va
3
3
G13
Gm11
C7♯5
3
F
A♭13
3
3
D♭7
3
G♭
G♭7♯9
8va
3
8vb
loco
F13
B9
B♭13
E13♯11

Am9
D13
D9♯5
Gm7
C/G
Gm9
C/G
Gm11
A7♭9/C♯
D7♯5(♯9)
G7♯5
Cm7
F7♯5(♭9)
B♭6
B♭m9
E♭9
A7♯5
D7♯5(♯9)
G13
Gm7
Gm7/C
F7♯5
Coda
B♭9
dim.
mp
Bdim7
F13/C
F13
F7♯5

B♭9
Bdim7
F7/C
C7♭9
F7♯5
B♭9
B7
C7
F7
B♭9
Bdim7
F6/C
F7♯5
B♭9
Bdim7

F/C
Cm9
F9
F9♯5
B♭9
Bdim7
F/C
C9
F7
B♭13
Bdim7
F6/C
A7♯5
D7♯5(♯9)
ff
8va
G9
Gm9
C7sus
F
N.C.
F13♯11
N.C.

Hello, Young Lovers

from *THE KING AND I*

Lyrics by Oscar Hammerstein II

Music by Richard Rodgers

N.C. Fm7
N.C. B♭7♭9
N.C. G♭maj7
B♭7♭9
N.C.
p
Swing
D♭13(add11)
mf
Tempo I
N.C.
8va
mp
(8va)
(8va)

(8va)
E♭5
G7♯5
loco
A♭13
3
Dm9
G13
Cm9
Fm7
D♭maj7♯5
G♭maj7♭5
8vb

8va
N.C.
Bass:
Piano:
loco
(8va)
(8va)
(8va)
E♭7
G7♯5
A♭m7
D9♭5
D♭9
(8va)
loco

C♭dim/G♭
E9(♭13)
D7♭5(♭9)
B♭7♯5(♯9)
B♭7♯5(♭9)
cresc.
E♭
N.C.
f
mp
Piano Solo: Chorus 1
E♭maj9
D♭9
4
2
G♭13
C♭9
Fm9
B♭7♯9

E♭6/9
Fm7/B♭
E♭6/9
D♭13♯11
G♭13
C♭9
Fm9
3
B♭7♯9
E♭6/9

A♭13
8va
(8va)
loco
G13
G7♯5
Cm9
Fm9
D♭maj7♯5
A♭9/G♭

Fm9
8va
B♭7♯5(♭9)
E♭maj9
loco
D♭13♯11
G♭13
C♭9
Fm9
F♭13♯11
E♭6/9
B♭13

Ensemble
Abmaj7
Db13#11
Eb/G
Gb13
N.C.
Stop time
G7#5
N.C.
f
Ab7
Db9
N.C.
Gb13
Cb7
N.C.
8vb
Cm7
N.C.
F
N.C.
(8vb)
Solo: Chorus 2
F13
Bb13
loco

A♭13
D♭9
E♭m7/A♭
D♭9
E♭m7/A♭
D♭9
G13
G7♯5
C9
C7♯9
F13
8va
B♭13
(8va)

(8va)
A♭13
(8va)
D♭9
E♭m7/A♭
loco
D♭9
E♭m7/A♭
D♭9
Gm7
C7♯9

F13
B♭13
A♭13
B♭13
A♭13
D♭9
A♭m7
D♭9
A♭m9
D♭9
C7♯9
F13

B♭13
A♭13
D♭9
A♭m7
D♭9
A♭m7
D♭9
G13(♯9)
G13(♭9)
C7♯5(♯9)
C7♯5(♭9)
Bridge
N.C. Fmaj9
N.C. Dmaj9
N.C. C♭maj9
N.C. A♭maj7
sub. p

Solo: G minor section

Gm7
C7
Gm7
3
C7
Gm7
C7
Gm7
C7
Gm7
C7
Gm7
C7
Gm7
3
3
3
Gm7
3
C7
8va

Gm7
C7
(8va)
loco
3
3
Gm7
C6
Gm7
Cm7(add4)
8va
Gm7
C7
Gm7
C7
(8va)
Gm7
C7
Gm7
C7
(8va)
Gm7
C6
Gm7
C6
(8va)

Gm7
C
Gm7
(8va)
C
Gm7
C
(8va)
Gm7
C
Gm7
(8va)
C
Gm7
(8va)
Gm7
C
Gm7
(8va)

C Gm7 C
(8va)
Gm7 C Gm7
(8va)
C7 Gm7 C7 Gm7
(8va)
C7 Gm7 C7 Gm7
(8va)
C7 Gm7 C7 Gm7
(8va)

C7
N.C. Gm7
C6
C13
C6
(8va)
C6
Gm7
N.C.
3
2
8
5
6

(8va)
2
5
8
(8va)
2
5
8
Gm7
3
3
C13
(8va)
3
(8va)
Gm7
C13
loco
Gm7
C6
Gm7
C6
Gm7
Begin fadeout...
2
2

C6
Gm7
C6
5
Gm7
C6
Gm7
2
2
4
2
C6
4
Gm7
C13
Gm7
8va
4
4
2
C13
(8va)
Gm7
loco
C13
Gm7
C6
Gm7
C6
Gm

We Kiss In A Shadow

from *THE KING AND I*

Lyrics by Oscar Hammerstein II

Music by Richard Rodgers

Fm7 Fm(maj7) Fm7 F9♭13 B♭13 B♭13♭9 E♭maj9 E♭6 A♭6
E♭maj9 Am7 D7 Gm7 Em7 A7 A7♭9
Dm6 G9 G7♭9 Cm Am7 D7
Gm7 F♯m7 Fm7 B♭13sus B♭13♭9
8va
E♭maj9 Fm7/E♭ B♭13♭9/E♭ E♭maj9 Edim Fm7 Fm(maj7)

Fm7 F9♭13 B♭9 Fdim E♭maj13 A7♭9 A♭6 Fm7 B♭7♭9
E♭maj9 Gm7♭5 B♭dim A7♭9 A♭6
Fm7 A7♭5 B♭13sus B♭13♭9 E♭maj13 Cm7 Fm7 B♭13♭9
Bass Solo
14
E♭maj7 Am13 D7♭9
A
Piano solo
Gm7 Em7 A7♭9

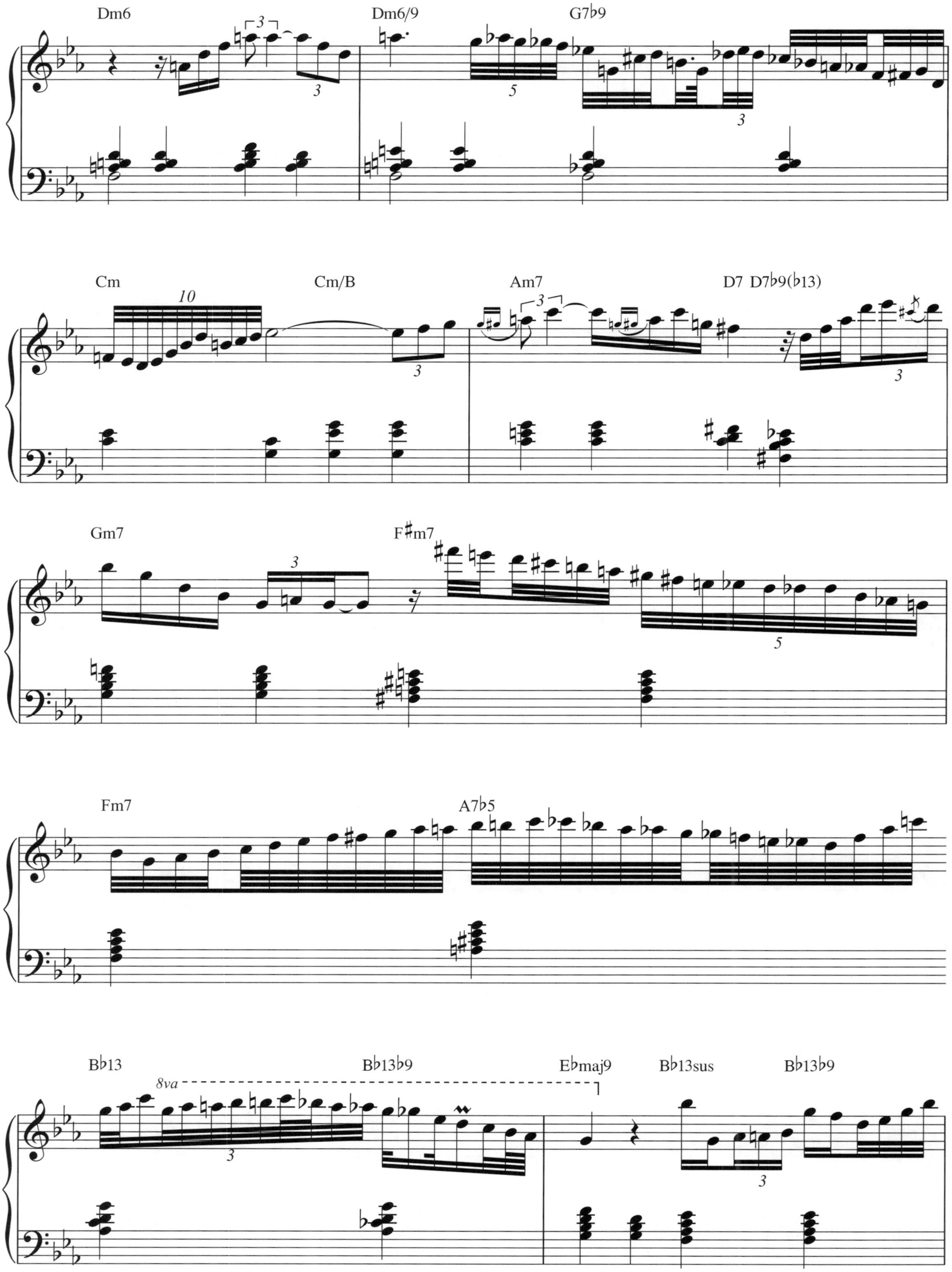
Dm6
Dm6/9
G7♭9
Cm
Cm/B
Am7
D7 D7♭9(♭13)
Gm7
F♯m7
Fm7
A7♭5
B♭13
8va
B♭13♭9
E♭maj9
B♭13sus
B♭13♭9

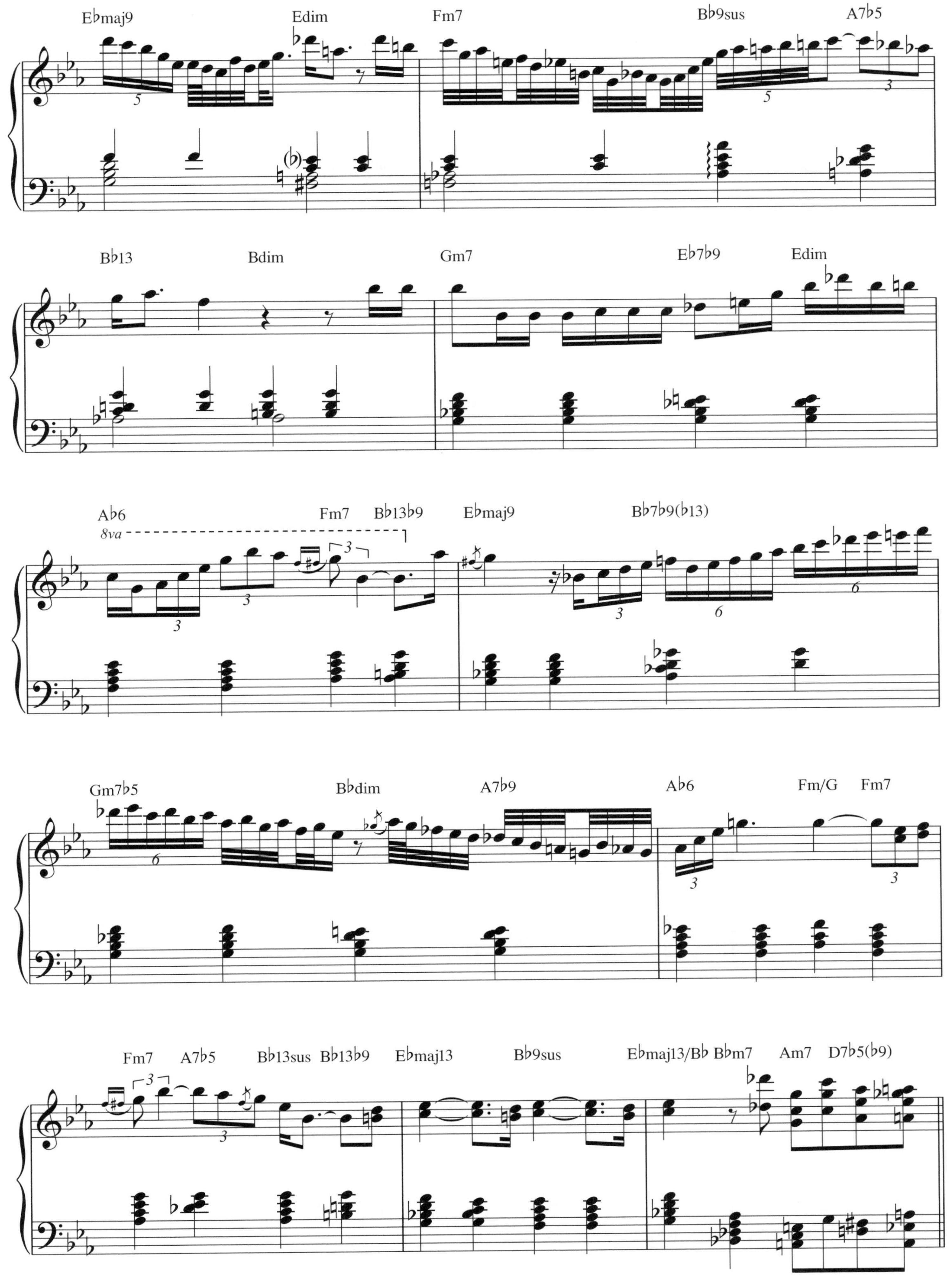
E♭maj9
Edim
Fm7
B♭9sus
A7♭5
B♭13
Bdim
Gm7
E♭7♭9
Edim
A♭6
8va
Fm7
B♭13♭9
E♭maj9
B♭7♭9(♭13)
Gm7♭5
B♭dim
A7♭9
A♭6
Fm/G
Fm7
Fm7
A7♭5
B♭13sus
B♭13♭9
E♭maj13
B♭9sus
E♭maj13/B♭
B♭m7
Am7
D7♭5(♭9)

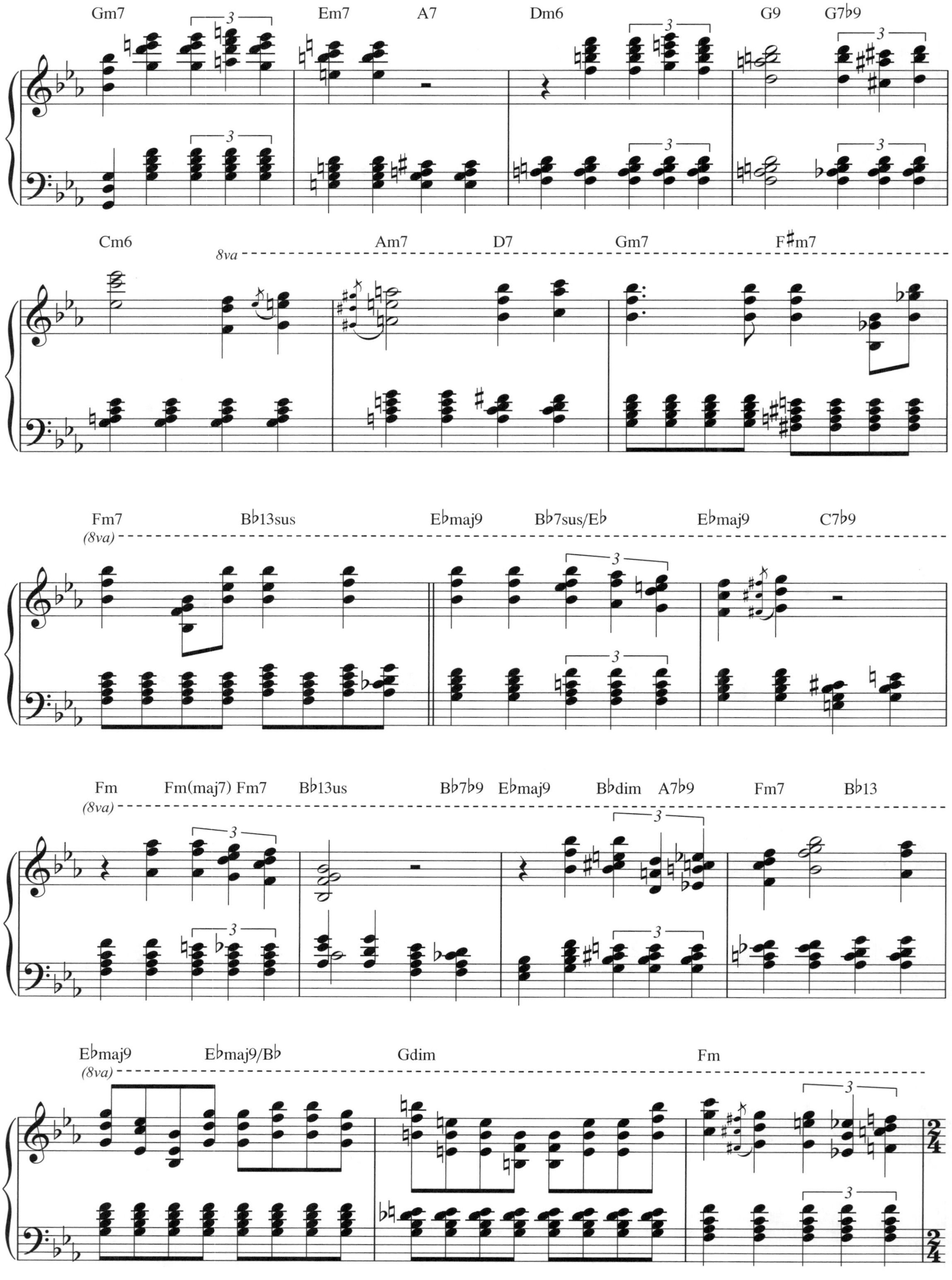
Gm7
Em7
A7
Dm6
G9
G7♭9
3
Cm6
8va
Am7
D7
Gm7
F♯m7
Fm7
(8va)
B♭13sus
E♭maj9
B♭7sus/E♭
E♭maj9
C7♭9
Fm
Fm(maj7)
Fm7
B♭13us
B♭7♭9
E♭maj9
B♭dim
A7♭9
Fm7
B♭13
E♭maj9
E♭maj9/B♭
Gdim
Fm

Moderately fast, very freely
B♭13sus
(8va)
8va
rit.
Faster
B♭13♭9
Gm7
Fm7
Gm7
Fm7
Gm7
8va
Fm7
Gm7
Fm7
Gm7
15ma
Fm7
Gm7
Fm7
8va
rit.
Gm7
(8va)
Fm7
Gm7
Fm7
Gm7
Fm7
Gm7
E♭maj13

I Have Dreamed

from *THE KING AND I*

Lyrics by Oscar Hammerstein II
Music by Richard Rodgers

Medium Swing (♩ = 192)

G6/D
D13sus
D7♭9
G6/D
D13sus
F7♯9
B♭13♭9
F7♯9 B♭13♭9
E♭maj7
A♭maj7♯11
G13
G7♭13
Cm7
G/B
B♭m7 Am7♭5
A♭m6
E♭/B♭
Adim A♭maj7
B♭dim
Cm7
F7♭9♯11
F♯dim
Gm7
Cdim/B♭
B♭13sus
F♭maj7
F♭7

B
B♭13sus
B♭7♭13
E♭dim/B♭
B♭7
E♭6/9
A/B♭
B♭7sus
C7/B♭
Fmaj7
C9sus
C9
Fm9
B♭13♭9
E♭6/9
Cm7
F7
B♭7sus
A♭13

Gmaj7
Gdim
D7♯9
G
Cmaj7
Fm9
B♭7♭9(♭13)
E♭7♯9
G7♭13
Cm7
F9
A♭m9
3
G7♭13
A♭
G7♭9
Cm7
F13
F♯dim
B♭7sus
8va

C
Cb13
Fm9
Fb6/9
Eb6/9
Fm
Bbm7
(8va)
Eb
Fm
Bb7b13
Eb6/9
(8va)
Gm
C7b9
Fm7
Bb13
F6/9
Gm7
C7b9
F6/9
Cm7
F7
Fm7
Ab13

G6
D7
Gdim
Gmaj13
Fm11
B♭7sus
B♭7♭13
E♭6/9
A♭
G7♭9(♭13)
Cm
Cm/B♭
A°
A♭m6
E♭/G
A♭maj7
G7♭13
Cm7
F13♯11
F♯dim

Gm11
G♭dim
Fm9
B♭13♭9
F♭maj7
D
E♭7♯9
Fm9
B♭7sus
E♭
Fm9
B♭7sus
(Bass solo ad lib.)
E♭
B♭7sus
B♭7♯11
F
B♭7♭9
E♭6/9
Cm
F7
B♭7
A♭9♯11
G

A7
D7sus
Gmaj7
Am
D7
Fm7
B♭7sus
E♭
A♭maj7
G7
Cm
Bm
B♭m
Am7
A♭m6
E♭/G
A♭7
G7♭9
Cm
F7♭9
F♯dim
Gm7
C7
Fm9
B♭7
F♭maj7♯11
E
E♭/B♭
B♭13sus
3
E♭/B♭
3
B♭13sus

Eb/Bb
Bb13sus
Fmaj13
C7sus
C9b6
F6/9
Fdim
Bb13
Eb6/9
Db7
C7#9
F13
Bb13sus
Ab13#11
G6
D13sus
Gdim/D
D13sus
D13b9
G6
D13sus
F7#9
Gb7#9
F7#9
Bb7sus
Bb13b9

Ebmaj13 Abmaj7#11 G7#5 Cm(maj9) Cm7 Cm6 Adim Abdim
Ebmaj7/Bb A13b9 Abmaj7 Bdim Cm7 F13#11 F#dim
Bb6 Cdim/Bb Fm9 Bb7b9 Cm7 F9#11 Gbdim
Eb/Bb Ebdim/Bb Bb9sus Fm6/9
Slowly, freely
Fbmaj13#11
8va

It Might As Well Be Spring

from *STATE FAIR*

Lyrics by OSCAR HAMMERSTEIN II

Music by RICHARD RODGERS

Moderately slow (𝅗𝅥 = 54)

Gb6/9
Gdim7
Dbmaj7/Ab
Bbm7
Ebm7
B7
Ab9
F7#9
Bb7
Eb7#9
Ab7
Db6/9/Ab
Gbmaj7/Ab
Gb7
Dbmaj7/Ab
Gbmaj7/Ab
swing eighths
Db6/9/Ab
A13
Gbmaj7/Ab
Db7
G13
Gbmaj7
Gdim7
Fm9
Bbm9

E♭m7
A13
A♭13
A♭m9
D♭9
G♭maj7
D♭sus/F
E♭9sus
A♭m9
D♭7
A♭m9
D♭9
G♭6/9
B♭m7
B♭9
E♭m9
D(♯5)
G♭6/D♭
Cm7♭5
F9
B♭m9
E♭9
E♭m9
Dmaj9♯11

D♭6/9
E♭m6/9
D♭6/9/A♭
A♭13
D♭6/9/A♭
A9♯5
A♭m9
D♭9
G6♭9
G♭maj9
C13♭9(♯11)
F7
B♭m
E♭m7
E♭m(maj7)
E♭m/D♭
Cm13♭5(♭9)
F7♭9(♯11)
E♭9
E♭m7♭5
A♭7♯5

Db6/9 F7#9 Bbm9 Bb/D Eb9 Ddim7
Db6/9/F Bbm7 Ebm9 Ab7
Db6/9/Ab Ab13 Db6/9/Ab
Ab13 Db6/9/Ab Ab7 Db6/9 E9/Ab
Eb9/Ab Ab7#5 Db6/9 A13

Abm9
Db7#9
Gbmaj9
Dbmaj7/Ab
Bbm9
Gbmaj9
A7
Ab7
Fm7
Bb7#5
Eb7#9
Ab7
Db6/9/Ab
A13
Ab13
Db6/9/Ab
A7/Ab
Ab7
Db6/9/Ab
A13

A♭m9
D♭7♯9
G♭maj9
Gdim7
D♭6/9/A♭
B♭m9
E♭m7
E♭7♯9
A♭7sus
A♭7♭9
A♭m9
D♭9sus
G♭6/9
E♭m7
A♭m7
D♭9
A♭m9

D♭11
D♭7
G♭maj7
B♭7♭9
E♭m9
G♭m7/D♭
G♭maj7♭5/C
F7♯5
B♭m9
E♭7♭9
E♭m9
Dmaj7
D♭maj7
A♭9
D♭6/9/A♭
A♭9

D♭6/9/A♭
A7
A♭m9
D♭7♯5(♯9)
G♭maj7
C7♭9(♯11)
D♭maj7/F
A6♭5
B♭m9
E♭m9
E♭m7/D♭
Cm11♭5
F7♭9(♯11)
E♭9
A13
E♭7♭5(♯9)
A♭7
D♭maj9
F7♯5(♯9)
B♭m9
E♭9
Gdim7

Fm7
B♭m9
E♭m9
A13
A♭11
D7♯9
D♭6/9/A♭
8va
A♭13
3
D♭6/9/A♭
(8va)
loco
A♭13
D♭6/9/A♭
3
3
A♭13
3
3
slower
D♭maj9
3

My Favorite Things

from *THE SOUND OF MUSIC*

Lyrics by Oscar Hammerstein II
Music by Richard Rodgers

B
Am
Asus
Am
Asus
Fmaj13
Fmaj7♯11
Fmaj13
Fmaj7♯11
Dm9
G7
Cmaj7
F6
C
C/B
Am
Am/G
F6
C/E
D♯dim
C
Am7

Fmaj7♯11
Dm13
G7
Cmaj7
F6
C
Bdim
A7sus
Am/G
Em/F
F/E
G/D
A♭/C
Fmaj7/B
B♭9
D
Am7
Dm9/A
E7/A
Am/G
C7/G
Fmaj7
A7♭9/E

Dm13
D7♭9(♯11)
D7♯9(♭13)
G13 G9sus
G13
G9sus
G7♭5(♭9)
G13♭9
E
C6/9
E♭7
A♭7
D♭maj7
C
Am7
D9
G13
F
Am
Am(♯5)
Am6
Am7

F
F6
D6
Dm7
G13
C6/9
Fmaj7
C6/9
Am
F
F/E
G
Am
Am(♯5)
Am6
Am7
F
F+
F6
F
F6
F

Dm7
G13
C6/9
F
C6/9
Am
F6
E7♭9
H
Am
Am(maj7)
Gdim/A
Fmaj7
E
Am
Am/G
Fmaj13
Em7
Edim
Dm
B♭7/D

G6
G9sus
G7♯9(♭13)
I
C9
E♭7
A♭maj7
D♭maj9
C
Am
D9
G13
J
Am7
Fmaj7

Dm7
G9
Cmaj7
F
Cmaj7
Am7
F
G13
K
Am7
Fmaj7
Dm7
G13
C6/9
Fmaj7

C6/9
B♭6/9
Am/E
Em7
C/E
E
L
Am7
Am(maj7)
Am
Dm7/A
Ddim/A
Am
Am/G
Fmaj13
Em7
Edim
Dm
D7♯5(♭9)
Am/G
A♭/G
G13♭9

*Piano: straight eighths. Bass and drums: continue swing feel..
†Full band: straight eighths.

Oh, What A Beautiful Mornin'

from *OKLAHOMA!*

Lyrics by Oscar Hammerstein II
Music by Richard Rodgers

F7♯5
Gdim
A7♯9
Bm7
E7
accel.
Quickly
B♭7sus
E♭6
Am7
D7
A♭7
D♭maj7
G♭maj7
C7♯5(♯9)
mf
Freely
8va
A7♯5(♯9)
F13
E9♭13
B7♭5(♭9)
E♭maj7♯2
G♭maj7♯2
G/A♭
Cm11
B
Moderately slow (♩ = 120)
G♭/F
Fmaj13

Fm13
B♭maj7/F
C
Slowly, freely
C♯dim/F
Fdim/C
F♯dim/F
C♯dim/F
B♭9sus
B♭/A♭
A♭/G♭
F/E♭
C/D♭
D♭/C
Bm7
F/B♭
Cm11
C7♯9
C♯dim/F
Bdim/C
To Coda
F♯dim/F
C♯dim/F
B♭maj7♯2
E13♭9
A7♯5(♯9)
D7♯9

Moderately slow (♩ = 80)
Gm13 D♭13 C9 Dm/E♭ A♭maj7 Dm/E♭
D
Moderately slow (♩ = 120)
A♭maj7 G♭/F Fmaj13
Fm13
E
B♭maj7/F F7
mf
B♭13 E7♭9 A7♯5(♯9)

D7♭5(♭9)
8va
G7♯5
C7
F7
Cm7
G♭6
F7
B♭7
A7
D7
Gm7
C7
Am7
A♭m7
F
Gm7
G♭7
8va
F7
D♭m
Cm7
F7
B♭7
B♭6
A7♯5

D7
A♭7
G13
C7♯9
F7
E♭7
Dm7
C♯dim
Cdim
C♭7
B♭13
E7♯9
B♭7
A7
D7
G7
C7
F7
E♭7
D7
D♭7
C7
G
F7
E♭7
Dm7
C7
C♭7
8va
B♭7
E7♯9
8vb

Am7
(8va)
D7♯5(♯9)
G7♯5
C7
F7
D♭m
Cm
F7
B♭
E7
B♭7
A7
D7
G7
C7
H
F
B♭dim
Adim
G7
G♭7
8va
F7
E♭7
Dm7
Cdim
C♭7
B♭13
E7♯9
Am7
8vb

D7♯9
G7♯5
C7♯9
8va
F
E♭
Dm
D♭m
Cm
B
B♭13
(8va)
E7♯9
A7
D7
G7
C7
F7
E7
A7
D7
D♭7
C
I
F
E♭
Dm
D♭m
Cm
C♭
B♭13
E7♯9
8va

A7
(8va)
A♭7
G7
C7
G♭7
F7
E♭7
Dm7
D♭dim
Cdim
B♭13
rit.
E7♯9
8va
Freely
A7♯5(♯9)
D7♯9
Gm13
C9
Moderately slow (♩ = 80)
Dm/E♭
A♭maj7
Dm/E♭
A♭maj7
D.S. al Coda
decresc.
CODA
A7♯5(♯9)
D7♯9
Gm13
D♭13
C9
A7♯5(♯9)
Dm7
F/A♭
cresc.

Gm13
D♭13
C9
D7♯9
Gm11
D♭13
C9
rit.
J
Moderately slow (♩ = 80)
Dm/E♭
A♭maj7
Dm/E♭
A♭maj7
p
Freely
A7♯5(♯9)
B7♯5(♯9)
G♭maj7♯2
C♭7♭9(♯11)
E♭maj7♯2
F/G♭
G/A♭
D♭6/C
G♭maj7♭5/F
8va
subf
Quickly, freely
(8va)
Fmaj13
8va
15ma
molto rit.

People Will Say We're In Love

from *OKLAHOMA!*

Lyrics by Oscar Hammerstein II
Music by Richard Rodgers

C
Am6
D9
Dm9
G7♯5
C6
Gdim
B
Dm7
G13♭5(♭9)
C6/9
Em7
A13♭9
Dm11
A♭m6/G
C
Em
Am

D13sus
D9
Dm9
G7♭5
C6/9
C
Cm9
F13
B♭maj13
E7♯9
A7♭5
D9
D
G7♭5(♭9)
C
F13
E7♯9

D13sus
D7♯5(♯9)
Em7
A7sus
Dm7
G7
C/G
D
C6/9
A7♭5
Dm9
G7sus
G7♯5
C6/9
D9
Dm9

G7♯5
C6/9
Dm6
G7
E
C6/9
E♭9
D9
G7sus
C
Am9
D13
8va
3
Dm9
(8va)
G7
C6/9

F
Cm7
F7
B♭
E7
A7
D7
G7♯5
C6/9
E7
Am9
D7♯9
D♯dim
C/E
A7♯5
D9
G7♯5
C/G
8va

G
C6/9
(8va)
A7♭5
Dm9
G7♯5
C6/9
Am9
D9
8va
Dm9
G7♯5
C6/9
G7♯5

H
C6/9
8va
A7
Dm7
G7
C6/9
D9
3
Dm9
G7sus
G7
C6/9

I
Cm7
F7
B♭
E7
A13
D7
G7sus
G7
C6/9
E7
Am9
D7♯9
C/E
A7♯5
D9
G7♯5
C
C/G

J
C6/9
Dm9
G13sus
G7♯5
C6/9
D9
Dm9
G7♯5
C6/9
A7♯5
Dm6
G7♯5
K
C6/9

8va
E♭m11
(8va)
Dm11
G13
C6/9
D9
Dm9
3
3
3
G7sus
G13
C6/9
L
Cm9
F13
C♭maj13
B♭maj13

E7
A13
D7
G7sus
G13♭5(♭9)
C6/9
F13♯11
E7
Am9
D7♯9
D♯dim
C/E
A7♯5
Dm9
G7♯5
M
C6/9
A7♭9
D7
G7
C
A7
D7

G7♯5 C9 A7♯5 D9
3 3
G7♯5 C9 A7♯5 D9
3
N
G7♯5 C9 A7♯5 D9
3
G7♯5 C9 A7♯5 D9
3 3 3 3
G7♯5 C9 A7♯5 D9
3 3 3

D♭maj13
Cmaj13
A7♯5(♭9)
D9
G7♯5
C13
A7♯5(♯9)
8va
O
D9
(8va)
G7♯5(♯9)
E7♯5(♯9)
A7♯5
(8va)
N.C.
Cmaj13
8vb

Shall We Dance?

from *THE KING AND I*

Lyrics by Oscar Hammerstein II
Music by Richard Rodgers

Fm Fm7 B♭7sus Gm7 G♭9 Fm9 F♭7♭5(♯5)
C
E♭ B♭9sus E♭maj7
D
A♭6 B♭9sus B♭7♭9
E♭ B♭9 Fm B♭7
E
E♭13 A♭6

E♭maj7
Gm7
C7♭9
Fm7
B♭7
E♭m7
Fm7
B♭7♭9
F
E♭
Edim
Fm7
B♭7
G
Fm7
B♭7
E♭/G
C7♯5(♯9)
F7♯9
E7♭5
E♭6
Cm
B♭7sus

Ebmaj7
Ab6
H
Bb9
Ebmaj7
Eb6
Bb7
Eb7
Bbm7
Eb7
I
Abmaj9
Ebmaj7
C7
Fm9
Bb13
Ebmaj7
C7#5(#9)
Fm7
Bb13

J
E♭
Edim
Fm7
B♭7
K
Fm7
B♭7
E♭/G
G♭9
Fm7sus
F♭13
3
L
E♭
E♭maj7
3
A♭6
3
M
B♭9sus
3
B♭7♭9
3

Ebmaj7
3
Bb9
Bb/Ab
Gm7
N
Bbm7
Eb7
Ab6
Eb
C7b9
Fm11
Bb9
O
Eb6
Eb7sus
Eb6
Eb7sus
Eb6
Eb7sus
Eb6
Abm/Eb
Eb6
Abm/Eb
Eb6
Abm/Eb
N.C.
Eb7#9

The Sound Of Music

from *THE SOUND OF MUSIC*

Lyrics by Oscar Hammerstein II
Music by Richard Rodgers

C/E
B♭maj7/F
Fm(maj7)♯5(♯11)
F/A
B♭/D
Am/C
C11
F6
F11
F7
B♭maj7
B♭dim7
F/C
Dm7
Gm7
C7♭9
F6/A
F6
F

B♭maj7
B♭dim7
F/A
Dm
G7sus
G7
C11
C7
B♭maj7
B♭m6
Am7
Dm7
Gm7
C7
Am7
Fmaj7
Dm(maj7)
Am7
C7♯5/G♯
Dm7
G13
Gm7
C11
C7♯5(♯9)

Fmaj13
Fm(maj7)♯5(♯11)
Fmaj7
B♭/D
B♭m7/D♭
8va
loco
F6/9/C
Cm7
F7
B♭maj7
Gm7♭5
Fmaj7/C
C11

F
B♭maj7 B♭/A
Gm7
F
Am7
Dm7
Gm7
C7
Fmaj7
Dm(maj7)
Am7(maj7)
Dm7
G13
Gm7
C13
E6
Emaj7

Em(maj7)♭5
Emaj7(13)/B
A/C♯
Am/C
Emaj7/B
Emaj7
E9
Amaj9
F♯m7♭5
Emaj7/B
B9
Emaj7/B B7
rit.
Freely
E
D
Cmaj9
Emaj7
Em(maj9)♭5
8va

The Surrey With The Fringe On Top

from *OKLAHOMA!*

Lyrics by Oscar Hammerstein II

Music by Richard Rodgers

B♭6/9 E♭ Dm7 G7♯9 C9sus C9
B
F13 B♭6/9 Gm7 Cm7 F7sus
B♭maj7 Gm9 Cm7 F7 B♭6/9 E♭
B♭/D Gm7 C9 F13sus F13
C
B♭9sus E♭6/9 Fm11 B♭13sus

E♭dim
E♭6/9
Gm9
C13sus
C7
F6/9
D7♯9
Gm11
C9
F13sus
F13
D
B♭
E♭/G
B♭maj7/F
E♭maj9
B♭maj7/D
B♭maj7/D♭
Cm11
F9sus
F7♭9
B♭
E♭
D7
G7
Cm7
G9sus
E♭m9
A♭13♯11
B♭/D
Gm7
3
Cm13
F13sus
F7♭9
B♭6/9

E
B♭
F13sus
F13
B♭
G7
Cm9
F7
B♭6
E♭7sus
D7♯9
G13
C9
F7sus
F7
F
B♭6
F7sus
B♭
G7
Cm9
F13
B♭
E♭7
D7
G13
C13
F9sus
F9
G
B♭13

E♭6/9
Fm9
B♭9
E♭6/9
Gm7
C9
F6/9
D7
Gm7
C7
8va
F13sus
3
H
B♭6/9
Cm7
F7
8va
B♭
G7♭13
3
Cm9
F13
B♭6/9
E♭maj7
D7♯9
G13
Cm9

E♭m9
A♭9sus
B♭/D
G7♭9
Cm9
F13
B♭6/9
F13sus
F13
I
B♭6/9
E♭maj7
E♭
B♭13sus
G13
Cm9
F13sus
F13
B♭
D7
G7
C9
F9sus
F13

J
B♭6/9
Gm9
8va
Cm7
F7
B♭
G7♭13
Cm9
F13
B♭6/9
D7♯9
Gm9
G7♭13
C9
3
F13sus
F13
K
B♭13sus
E♭
Fm9
B♭13
E♭dim
E♭6/9
Gm9
C7
Fmaj7
D7♯9

L
Gm9 C13 F13sus F13 B♭6/9 E♭/G
B♭maj7/F E♭/G B♭ Gm9 Cm9 F13 B♭maj7 D7
M
Dm7 G13 Cm9 Dm7 E♭m9 A♭ D7♯9 G7♯9
Cm9 F7♭9 Dm7 Gm7 Gm/C Dm/F B♭/D G7♭13
Cm9 F7♭9 B♭ Fm7 Em7 E♭m9 Dm9 D♭m9 Cm9 B♭maj9♯11
rit.

This Nearly Was Mine

from *SOUTH PACIFIC*

Lyrics by Oscar Hammerstein II
Music by Richard Rodgers

F♯/A♯
Am6
G♯m7
G♯m6
G6
B/F♯
Fm7♭5
Emaj7
Em6
Bmaj7/D♯
F♯7
8vb
B
B6
accel.
Faster
Bm7♭5
B

Moderately fast, expressively
G/B
rit.
B
C♯m11
Ddim
Bmaj7/D♯
F♯/A♯
Am6
Emaj7/G♯
G6
B/F♯
Fm7
Emaj13
8vb
C♯m7♭5
B/F♯
F♯7sus
F♯7
Moderately, steadily (♩ = 132)
B

B7♭9(♭13)
Emaj7
F♯dim
Emaj7/G♯
F♯/A♯
F♯7
B
C♯m7♭5
F♯7/C♯
B
Adim
E/G♯
F♯13sus
F♯dim
E
D♯
D
C♯
D♯m
E
F♯
F♯7
B
C♯m7

Ddim
B/D♯
F♯/A♯
Adim
Emaj7/G♯
Em(maj7)/G
B/F♯
Fm7♭5
E
C♯7♯5
B/F♯
F♯7sus
B
F7♭9
B♭
Cm
Cm6
B♭/D
G7♭9
C7♭9
F7♭9

B♭13♭9
B♭7♭13(♭9)
E♭maj13
E♭m
B♭/F
F
Gm9
Em7♭5
E♭m7
B♭/D
D♭dim
Cm7
F7
B♭
F7
B♭
Cm
C♯dim

B♭/D
F/A
A♭dim
E♭maj7/G
G♭7♯9
G♭9
B♭maj7/F
Em7♭5
E♭maj7
Cm7♭5
F
F7
B♭
E♭
B♭7/F
E♭/B♭
Cm7
F7
8vb

Bb
Bb7b5(b9)
Ebmaj7
Fdim
Eb/G
C13
F9
Eb9
Db9
Cb9
A9
G9
F9

B♭maj7
Cm6
D♭dim
B♭maj7/D
8va
F/A
A♭dim
(8va)
E♭/G
E♭m6/G♭
B♭/F
Em7♭5
E♭maj13
C13
B♭/F
F+
F9
B♭
Cm7
C♯dim
B♭/D
Edim
Fm6

(♩♩ = ♩♪ 3)
E♭/G
Fdim
E♭6
Am7♭5/E♭
B♭/D
Cm6
3
3
3
B♭7
A♭6
E♭/G
Fm6
E♭6
B♭/D
E♭
B♭13
3
E♭/G
C
B♭/D
C/E
F
Gm
F/A
F
3

F♯7
8vb
8va
rit.
(8vb)
Slowly, freely
B
C♯m11
Ddim
B/D♯
F♯/A♯
Adim
Emaj7/G♯
Em(maj7)/G
B/F♯
F13♯11

Emaj7
Db7b5(b9)
B/F#
F#9sus
B
B7b9
E
Em6
B/F#
Fm7b5
Amaj7/E
Am7b5/Eb
G#m7/D#
C#m7b5
Em/F#
F#7
B
8vb

Younger Than Springtime

from *SOUTH PACIFIC*

Lyrics by Oscar Hammerstein II
Music by Richard Rodgers

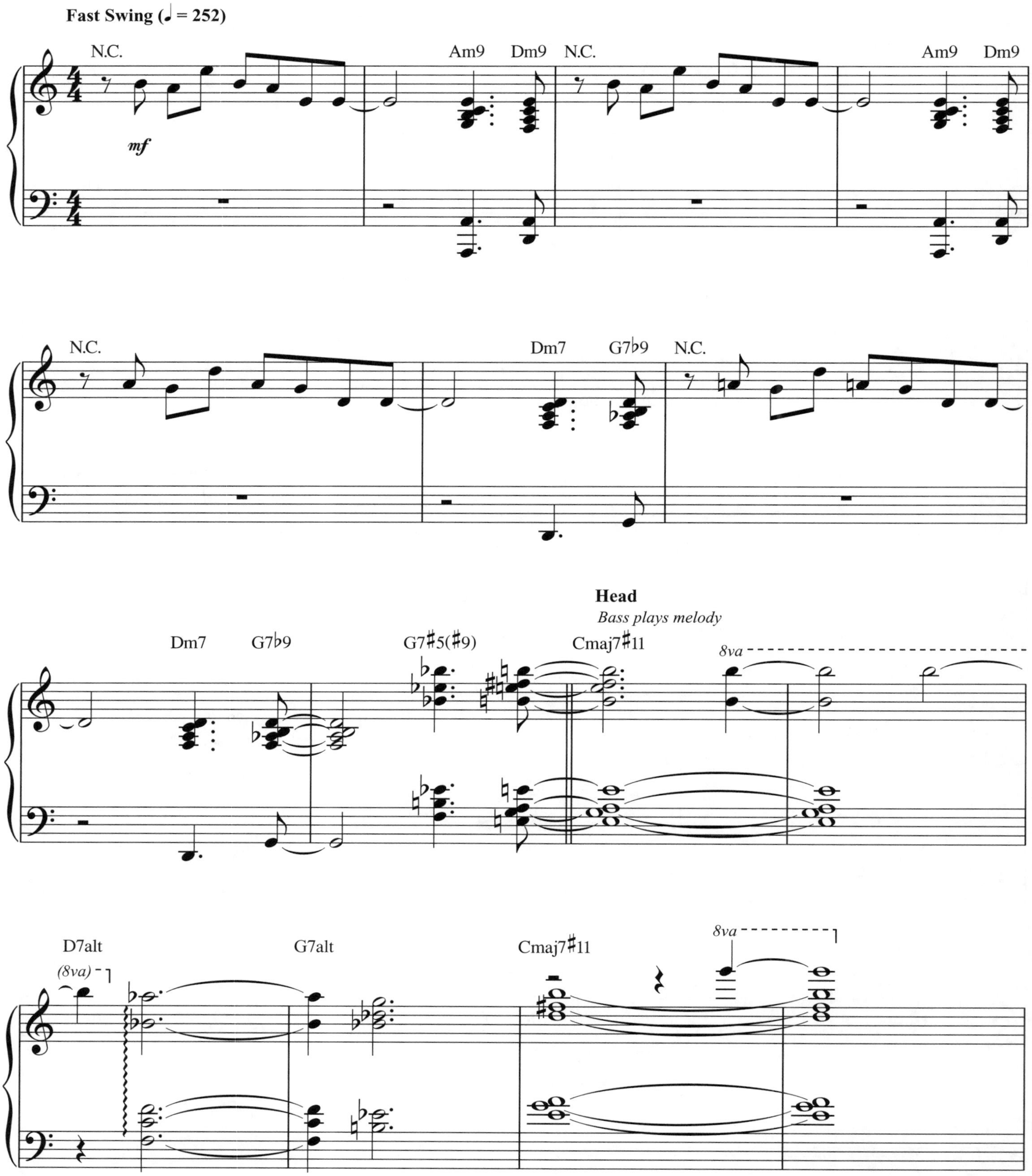

D7
G7
Cmaj7
D7alt
G7alt
Cmaj13
8va
D7
A7
D7
G/B
E7
Am7
D7
G7
Em7
Am7
D7
G
Dm7
G7
Cmaj7

D7alt
15ma
G7alt
Cmaj13
D9
Fm7
Piano fills
Cmaj7/G
G7♭9(♭13)
Cmaj7/G
G7♭9(♭13)
Piano solo
C
F7
E7
A7
Dm7
A♭7
G7

C F7 E7 A7 D7 G7♯5(♯9)
C F7 E7 A7 D7 G7
C F7 E7 A7 Am7 D7 G7
A7 D7 B7 E7 A7 Dm7 B7 E7
A7 Dm7 G Dm7 G7

Cmaj9
F13
Em7
B♭6
A7♭13
Dm9
A♭13
G13
A♭13
G13
C
F7
Em7
Am7
F♯m7♭5
Fm6
8va
Cmaj7/G
(8va)
G7♯5(♯9)
3
(8va)
Cmaj7/G
G7♯5(♯9)
Cmaj7

G
C
F7
E7
A7
D7
G7
C
3
F7
E7
A7
D7
G7♯9
8va
C
F
E7
A7
Dm7
3
D7
G7
C
F7
E7
A7

D7
G
A7
D7
B7
E7
A7
D7
G7
E7
A7
D7
G
Dm7
G7
C
F7
Em7
A7
Dm7
G7
C
F7
Em7
Am7
F♯m7♭5
Fm9

Em7
A7
Dm7
G7
C
A7
D7
G7
C
F7
Em7
A7
D7
G7
C
F
Em7
A7
D7
G7
C
F7
E7
A7
D7
G7
C
F
Em7
Am7
D7
G
E7
8va

A7 D7 B7 E7 A7 D7
G7 A7 D7 G
Dm7 G7 C F7 Em7 A7
Dm7 G7 C F7
C/E Am7 F♯m7♭5 Fm9 Em7 A7
8va

Dm7 G7 C A7 D7 G7
Bass solo
C F7 E7 A7
34
36
34
36
Piano solo
C7 F7 E7 A7 D7 G7
C7 F7 E7 A7 D7 G7
C F7 Em7 A7 Dm7
3
3
3
3

G7 C F7 Em7 A7
D7 G A7 D7
B7 E7 A7sus D7 G7 E7
A7 D7 G Dm7 G7
C F7 Em7 A7 Dm7 G7

C F7 Em7 Am7 F♯m7♭5
3 3 3 3 3
Fm9 Em7 A7 Dm7 G7 C A7
8vb
Dm7 G7 C F7 Em7 Am7 Dm7
(♭) 3 (♮)
(8vb)
G7 C F7 E7 A7 D7
A
G7♯9 C F Em Am7

Dm7
G7
C
F
Em7
A7sus
D7
G
Am7
D7
E♭m7
Em7
Am7
F♯6
G6
E13♭9
Am7
D7
E♭m7
Em7
Dm7
G7♯5(♯9)
Bass plays melody
Cmaj13♯11
D7♯9(♭5)
G13♯9
Cmaj13

Piano solo
D7/F♯
Fm13
Cmaj7/G
G7♭9(♭13)
Cmaj7/G
G7♭9(♭13)
8va
(8va)
Cmaj7
F13
Em7
A7♭5(♭9)
Dm11
D♭5
Cmaj13♯11
15ma
8vb

ARTIST TRANSCRIPTIONS®

Artist Transcriptions are authentic, note-for-note transcriptions of today's hottest artists in jazz, pop and rock. These outstanding, accurate arrangements are in an easy-to-read format which includes all essential lines. **Artist Transcriptions** can be used to perform, sequence or for reference.

CLARINET

00672423 Buddy De Franco Collection ... $19.95

FLUTE

00672379 Eric Dolphy Collection ... $19.95
00672582 The Very Best of James Galway ... $16.99
00672372 James Moody Collection – Sax and Flute ... $19.95

GUITAR & BASS

00660113 The Guitar Style of George Benson ... $14.95
00699072 Guitar Book of Pierre Bensusan ... $29.95
00672331 Ron Carter – Acoustic Bass ... $16.95
00672573 Ray Brown ... $19.99
00672307 Stanley Clarke Collection ... $19.95
00660115 Al Di Meola – Friday Night in San Francisco ... $14.95
00604043 Al Di Meola – Music, Words, Pictures ... $14.95
00672574 Al Di Meola – Pursuit of Radical Rhapsody ... $22.99
00125617 Best of Herb Ellis ... $19.99
00673245 Jazz Style of Tal Farlow ... $19.95
00699306 Jim Hall – Exploring Jazz Guitar ... $19.95
00604049 Allan Holdsworth – Reaching for the Uncommon Chord ... $14.95
00699215 Leo Kottke – Eight Songs ... $14.95
00672353 Joe Pass Collection ... $18.95
00673216 John Patitucci ... $16.95
00027083 Django Reinhardt Antholog ... $14.95
00672374 Johnny Smith Guitar Solos ... $19.99

PIANO & KEYBOARD

00672338 Monty Alexander Collection ... $19.95
00672487 Monty Alexander Plays Standards ... $19.95
00672520 Count Basie Collection ... $19.95
00113680 Blues Piano Legends ... $19.99
00672439 Cyrus Chestnut Collection ... $19.95
00672300 Chick Corea – Paint the World ... $12.95
14037739 Storyville Presents Duke Ellington ... $19.99
00146105 Bill Evans – Alone ... $16.99
00672537 Bill Evans at Town Hall ... $16.95
00672548 The Mastery of Bill Evans ... $12.95
00672425 Bill Evans – Piano Interpretations ... $19.95
00672365 Bill Evans – Piano Standards ... $19.95
00121885 Bill Evans – Time Remembered ... $19.99
00672510 Bill Evans Trio – Vol. 1: 1959-1961 ... $24.95
00672511 Bill Evans Trio – Vol. 2: 1962-1965 ... $24.99
00672512 Bill Evans Trio – Vol. 3: 1968-1974 ... $24.95
00672513 Bill Evans Trio – Vol. 4: 1979-1980 ... $24.95
00672381 Tommy Flanagan Collection ... $24.99
00672492 Benny Goodman Collection ... $16.95
00672486 Vince Guaraldi Collection ... $19.95
00672419 Herbie Hancock Collection ... $19.95
00672438 Hampton Hawes ... $19.95
14037738 Storyville Presents Earl Hines ... $19.99
00672322 Ahmad Jamal Collection ... $22.95
00672564 Best of Jeff Lorber ... $17.99
00672476 Brad Mehldau Collection ... $19.99
00672388 Best of Thelonious Monk ... $19.95
00672389 Thelonious Monk Collection ... $19.95
00672390 Thelonious Monk Plays Jazz Standards – Volume 1 ... $19.95
00672391 Thelonious Monk Plays Jazz Standards – Volume 2 ... $19.95
00672433 Jelly Roll Morton – The Piano Rolls ... $12.95
00672553 Charlie Parker for Piano ... $19.95
00672542 Oscar Peterson – Jazz Piano Solos ... $16.95
00672562 Oscar Peterson – A Jazz Portrait of Frank Sinatra ... $19.95
00672544 Oscar Peterson – Originals ... $10.99
00672532 Oscar Peterson – Plays Broadway ... $19.95
00672531 Oscar Peterson – Plays Duke Ellington ... $19.95
00672563 Oscar Peterson – A Royal Wedding Suite ... $19.99
00672569 Oscar Peterson – Tracks ... $19.99
00672533 Oscar Peterson – Trios ... $24.95
00672543 Oscar Peterson Trio – Canadiana Suite ... $12.99
00672534 Very Best of Oscar Peterson ... $22.95
00672371 Bud Powell Classics ... $19.95
00672376 Bud Powell Collection ... $19.95
00672507 Gonzalo Rubalcaba Collection ... $19.95
00672303 Horace Silver Collection ... $19.95
00672316 Art Tatum Collection ... $22.95
00672355 Art Tatum Solo Book ... $19.95
00673215 McCoy Tyner ... $17.99
00672321 Cedar Walton Collection ... $19.95
00672519 Kenny Werner Collection ... $19.95
00672434 Teddy Wilson Collection ... $19.95

SAXOPHONE

00672566 The Mindi Abair Collection ... $14.99
00673244 Julian "Cannonball" Adderley Collection ... $19.95
00673237 Michael Brecker ... $19.95
00672429 Michael Brecker Collection ... $19.95
00672315 Benny Carter Plays Standards ... $22.95
00672394 James Carter Collection ... $19.95
00672349 John Coltrane Plays Giant Steps ... $19.95
00672529 John Coltrane – Giant Steps ... $14.99
00672494 John Coltrane – A Love Supreme ... $14.95
00307393 John Coltrane – Omnibook: C Instruments ... $24.99
00307391 John Coltrane – Omnibook: B-flat Instruments ... $24.99
00307392 John Coltrane – Omnibook: E-flat Instruments ... $24.99
00307394 John Coltrane – Omnibook: Bass Clef Instruments ... $24.99
00672493 John Coltrane Plays "Coltrane Changes" ... $19.95
00672453 John Coltrane Plays Standards ... $19.95
00673233 John Coltrane Solos ... $22.95
00672328 Paul Desmond Collection ... $19.95
00672379 Eric Dolphy Collection ... $19.95
00672530 Kenny Garrett Collection ... $19.95
00699375 Stan Getz ... $19.95
00672377 Stan Getz – Bossa Novas ... $19.95
00672375 Stan Getz – Standards ... $18.95
00673254 Great Tenor Sax Solos ... $18.99
00672523 Coleman Hawkins Collection ... $19.95
00673252 Joe Henderson – Selections from "Lush Life" & "So Near So Far" ... $19.95
00672330 Best of Joe Henderson ... $22.95
00672350 Tenor Saxophone Standards ... $18.95
00673239 Best of Kenny G ... $19.95
00673229 Kenny G – Breathless ... $19.95
00672462 Kenny G – Classics in the Key of G ... $19.95
00672485 Kenny G – Faith: A Holiday Album ... $14.95
00672373 Kenny G – The Moment ... $19.95
00672498 Jackie McLean Collection ... $19.95
00672372 James Moody Collection – Sax and Flute ... $19.95
00672416 Frank Morgan Collection ... $19.95
00672539 Gerry Mulligan Collection ... $19.95
00672352 Charlie Parker Collection ... $19.95
00672561 Best of Sonny Rollins ... $19.95
00102751 Sonny Rollins with the Modern Jazz Quartet ... $17.99
00675000 David Sanborn Collection ... $17.95
00672491 New Best of Wayne Shorter ... $19.95
00672550 The Sonny Stitt Collection ... $19.95
00672350 Tenor Saxophone Standards ... $18.95
00672567 The Best of Kim Waters ... $17.99
00672524 Lester Young Collection ... $19.95

TROMBONE

00672332 J.J. Johnson Collection ... $19.95
00672489 Steve Turré Collection ... $19.99

TRUMPET

00672557 Herb Alpert Collection ... $16.99
00672480 Louis Armstrong Collection ... $17.95
00672481 Louis Armstrong Plays Standards ... $17.95
00672435 Chet Baker Collection ... $19.95
00672556 Best of Chris Botti ... $19.95
00672448 Miles Davis – Originals, Vol. 1 ... $19.95
00672451 Miles Davis – Originals, Vol. 2 ... $19.95
00672450 Miles Davis – Standards, Vol. 1 ... $19.95
00672449 Miles Davis – Standards, Vol. 2 ... $19.95
00672479 Dizzy Gillespie Collection ... $19.95
00673214 Freddie Hubbard ... $14.95
00672382 Tom Harrell – Jazz Trumpet ... $19.95
00672363 Jazz Trumpet Solos ... $9.95
00672506 Chuck Mangione Collection ... $19.95
00672525 Arturo Sandoval – Trumpet Evolution ... $19.95

HAL•LEONARD® CORPORATION
7777 W. Bluemound Rd. P.O. Box 13819 Milwaukee, WI 53213

Visit our web site for a complete listing of our titles with songlists at
www.halleonard.com

Prices and availability subject to change without notice.